WINDERMERE

John Morrison

HALSGROVE

First published in Great Britain in 2008

Copyright © 2008 John Morrison

British Library Cataloguing-in-Publication Data
A CIP record for this title is available from the British Library

ISBN 978 1 84114 717 8

HALSGROVE
Halsgrove House
Ryelands Industrial Estate
Bagley Road, Wellington, Somerset TA21 9PZ
Tel: 01823 653777   Fax: 01823 216796
email: sales@halsgrove.com
website: www.halsgrove.com

Printed and bound by Grafiche Flaminia, Italy

Contents

How to use this book

There are some terrific walks around Windermere, and, even on the busiest of bank holidays, the surrounding fells are unlikely to be crowded. Hardcore hikers head for the higher fells, you see, while a lot of visitors to Windermere seem to regard the ascent of Bowness Hill as the height of their ambitions, popping into a teashop whenever tannin deprivation kicks in. So you can walk out of Bowness, Windermere or Ambleside and, within a very few minutes, be out on the breezy tops — enjoying panoramic views of the lake and the company of ravens and buzzards.

At 11 miles, Windermere is England's longest lake, and only Wastwater is deeper. The lake shows two very different faces to the world; it's almost as though there are two Windermeres. The eastern side is mostly in private hands, which limits access to the lakeshore to just a few locations, such as Waterhead, Bowness Bay and Fell Foot Park. The western shore, in contrast, has a more open aspect, and is accessible to walkers for much of its length.

Windermere changes dramatically from north to south as well, a transformation that's particularly striking when the lake is viewed from the top of Wansfell (walk 1). Look south — to the left — to see the low-lying Silurian hills, descending to the shifting sands of Morecambe Bay. Look north — to the right — to see the major peaks of central Lakeland, formed from Borrowdale Volcanic rock.

The walks in this little book may whet your appetite for the more dramatic scenery to the north, though for sheer variety of landscape Windermere is hard to beat. When you climb one of the high peaks, you can trudge for an hour uphill without much change of view, but around Windermere the scenery is constantly changing. It's an intimate landscape, and I like it a lot.

These ten walks offer a great deal of variety — exploring the lake shore, the frieze of surrounding fells and visiting some fascinating places on the way. The walks are all relatively easy, both in terms of route-finding and the wear and tear on a walker's knees. Nevertheless, I wouldn't recommend doing any walking without the appropriate OS map.

Conveniently, all ten walks appear on the double-sided Ordnance Survey Explorer map OL7: The English Lakes, south eastern area. The maps in this book offer just a schematic version of each walk, while the OS map puts the routes into their true landscape context. Loughrigg Fell (walk 10), for example, is criss-crossed with so many paths that describing one definitive route is impossible. On terrain like this, an OS map is invaluable.

The walks are evenly spread around the lake, going clockwise from Ambleside. My favourites? Well, the view of the lake from Wansfell (walk 1) is hard to beat and Loughrigg Fell (walk 10) offers a tantalising glimpse of bigger Lakeland scenery. But if you want a great view, with minimum effort, and have only a couple of hours to spare, then I'd plump for a brisk scramble up Gummer's How (Walk 5).

My favourite buildings are Town End, in Troutbeck (walk 1) and St Anthony's Church at Cartmel Fell (walk 5). My least favourite building ought to be Wray Castle (walk 9) for being so ridiculous and out of place. But I'd probably miss it if it wasn't there. The urge to build inappropriate dwellings is still with us, as witnessed by some of the uglier buildings in Bowness and the vainglorious mansions on the eastern shore of the lake.

Half of the walks (1,4, 6, 8 & 10) visit pubs on the way. Other pubs worth seeking out include the Masons Arms at Strawberry Bank, the Drunken Duck near Ambleside and the Hole in't Wall, Bowness. All three take a bit of finding, though plenty of people seem to manage it. The Wateredge Hotel, at the northern tip of the lake, is easier to find, and, as its name suggests, it has a beer garden that goes down to the water.

Public transport in the area ranges from dreadful to dire. When Alfred Wainwright wrote his seven Guides to the Fells, he did it all by public transport. Amazing. There *are* buses, but they're infrequent. Stagecoach North West runs the Cumbria Rider Service. Timetables are available from the Tourist Information Centres in Bowness, Windermere and Ambleside, or phone 0871-2002233. Northern Rail run a good service of trains from Oxenholme, on the West Coast main line, to Windermere station. Get a timetable from the station or one of the TICs; website listed on page 7.

Windermere Ferry runs daily between Ferry Nab, just south of Bowness, and Ferry House, on the western side of the lake. From April to October expect the ferry to run every 20 minutes, from 6.50am-9.50pm on weekdays (9.10am-9.50pm on Sundays). From November to March: 6.50am-8.50pm on weekdays (9.50am-8.50pm on Sundays). Foot passengers and up to 18 cars can be accommodated on each crossing. Further information: 01228-607653.

Windermere Lakes Cruises operates the passenger boats on the lake, linking Ambleside, Bowness and Lakeside (phone for a timetable: 015394-43360). This is a wonderful way to see the lake, especialy when a boat trip is combined with one of these walks, or a ride on the Lakeside-Haverthwaite Steam Railway.

Useful websites...

Lake District National Park
www.lake-district.gov.uk

Cumbria Tourist Board
www.cumbria-the-lake-district.co.uk

Cumbria Tourism
www.golakes.co.uk

The Windermere Way (a 45-mile
circular walk around the lake)
www.windermere-way.co.uk

Windermere Lake Cruises Ltd
www.windermere-lakecruises.co.uk

Northern Rail
www.northernrail.org

Lake District Outdoors
www.lakedistrictoutdoors.co.uk

Lakeside Haverthwaite steam railway
www.lakesiderailway.co.uk

True North Photography
www.northpix.co.uk

Walk Locations

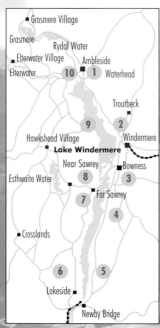

Key to Symbols Used

Level of difficulty:

Easy 🐛

Fair 🐛 🐛

More challenging 🐛 🐛 🐛

Map symbols:

Tarred Road	——
Footpath	- - - - -
Building	■
Church	+
Pub	🍺

1 Wansfell and Troutbeck

Enjoy matchless views of the lake, on this exhilarating walk, and return on an old drovers' track

Level: ♥ ♥ ♥

Length: 6 miles

Terrain: A steep haul up to the top of Wansfell, with a less strenuous return from Troutbeck on good tracks.

Websites: Consider combining this walk with a visit to Town End, a fine National Trust property in Troutbeck www.nationaltrust.org.uk

You need to gain height to see Windermere in its landscape context, and few vantage points offer a better opportunity than the rocky summit of Wansfell. With a height of only 484m, Wansfell is no match for the peaks of central Lakeland; nevertheless the views are both extensive and breathtaking. Ambleside looks like a model village; boats on the lake seem no bigger than toys.

The walk descends into the Troutbeck valley. Not one of those villages that huddles around a green, Troutbeck straggles along both sides of the valley – farms and houses keeping a respectful distance from their neighbours. While Ambleside is essentially a creation of the Victorian era, Troutbeck has a much older heritage, with characterful buildings dating back to the 17th century.

The most interesting house is Town End, built in 1623 by George Browne, a prominent yeoman farmer. The house remained in the Browne family until 1943, and is now looked after by the National Trust. With its original oak panelling and furniture, the interior of the

RT eside

Waterfall

2 3

4 5

Wansfell Summit

Mortal Man Pub

11

High Skelghyll Farm

9

Troutbeck 6

10

Jenkin Crag

7

8

9

house is wonderfully evocative of a time long gone.

 At the top end of Ambleside is the Salutation Hotel. Take a narrow road just to the right of the hotel, between a bank and the old market hall. When the road bears left, uphill, signs confirm that this is the route for Stock Ghyll Waterfall and Wansfell Pike. Soon you're leaving the bustle of Ambleside behind, as you follow Stock Ghyll Beck uphill (you'll soon need to make a short detour, to the left, if you want to see Stock Ghyll Force: an impressive sight, especially after rain).

Stock Ghyll waterfall

Continue up the road; as the view begins to open out, look for a rather elaborate double stile on the right, signed as a footpath to Troutbeck via Wansfell.

A good track leads uphill, accompanying a beck.

Through a gate, your path is now on stone steps: a fine example of how a well-used footpath can be repaired without making it a blot on the landscape. Your way to the top of

Windermere from Wansfell

Wansfell is clear. Cross a little footbridge to leave the beck behind, to climb above the tree line. Go through a gap in a wall, and up to the rocky top of Wansfell.

As a name for a pub, the Mortal Man is probably unique. When a local artist painted a new sign for the pub, originally the White House, around 1800, he included this doggerel:

Oh Mortal Man that lives by bread
What is it makes thy nose so red?
Thou silly fool, that looks so pale,
T'is drinking Sally Birkett's ale.

(4) This is the perfect spot to sit down, open your sandwiches and enjoy the view. And what a view it is: a 360-degree panorama. Kirkstone Pass (plus inn and slate quarry), Fairfield, Grasmere and Rydal, the Langdales, the Coniston range and beyond, with Windermere stretched out below like a ribbon of silver. Cross a ladder stile to take an obvious path ahead, steadily downhill towards the Troutbeck valley. As Windermere fades from view, go through two kissing gates to reach a walled track, known as Nanny Lane.

(5) Go right, along the track. Cross a stile and continue downhill, more steeply now, as you reach Troutbeck (go left here for refreshments at the Mortal Man pub).

(6) To continue the walk, go right, along the road, passing some of the characterful houses in this ancient village, and St John's Well. Where a road bears off to the left, there's a Post Office on the right (for Town End, continue along the road).

(7) Bear right here, uphill, onto Robin Lane (a sign on the wall of the Post Office points the way: 'Footpath via Skelghyll and Jenkin Crag to Ambleside'). Beyond a couple of houses the road becomes a stoney track. Soon, the middle reaches of Windermere come into view once again. It's easy walking, mostly on the level, along this walled track, which skirts the lower slopes of Wansfell. As you lose the lake view, you come to a fork of tracks, both gated.

Windermere from Robin Lane

 Keep left, as the track descends; through two small gates, across a stream, you reach a metalled track. Go right here, uphill, over a cattle grid, as a sign confirms

this is a public bridleway to Ambleside.

 Go throught the farmyard of High Skelghyll Farm and

take a gate beyond the farmhouse, through another gate and onto a level track, with good views of Windermere. Low Wood Hotel and marina are in the foreground.

Town End, Troutbeck

10 Descend through deciduous woodland, looking out for a hole in the wall on your left and a National Trust sign (make a slight detour here if you want to view the lake from Jenkin Crag). Continue downhill, through woodland, keeping right where the track forks (the track on the left would take you down to Waterhead and the lake). Zig-zag downhill to join a more substantial track, and arrive back in Ambleside by Hayes Garden Centre.

11 Avoid the main road by walking, right, along the Old Lake Road, and back into the centre of town.

Walkers in Troutbeck

View from Orrest Head

2 **Orrest Head**

Enjoy the view that inspired Alfred Wainwright
to leave Blackburn and move to the Lake District

Alfred Wainwright was just 23 years old when he first visited the Lake District. Born and raised in the Lancashire milltown of Blackburn, he was unprepared for what he found.

"That week changed my life", he wrote years later. "It was the first time that I'd looked upon beauty"

Wainwright arrived by train; his moment of epiphany came just a few minutes later when he viewed Lake Windermere from the vantage point of Orrest Head. He was transfixed. "Those few hours on Orrest Head left a spell that changed my life". In the years that followed, Wainwright got to know the Lake District rather better, of course, as he compiled his Guides to the Fells, but he never forgot his first sight of Windermere.

There can be few vantage points which offer such a splendid reward for such little effort. It takes just 20 minutes to

Level:
Length: 2 ½ miles
Terrain: Easy walking, except for the steep approach to Orrest Head.
Park & start: Park in Windermere town; there's a pay & display car park in Broad Street (GR NY413983)
Websites: www.wainwright.org.uk

walk from the railway station, through woodland and up to the rocky outcrop of Orrest Head. And what a view it is: England's longest lake, cradled by hills, with the sands of Morecambe Bay glistening on the southern horizon, and, to the north, the craggy peaks of central Lakeland.

Causeway Farm ■

Low Hag Wood
5
4

6

Cairn • Orrest Head
2 ▲
3

Windermere
7
1

START ■ Windermere Railway Station

Pathway back to Windermere

1 Walk up to the top of the town, cross the busy A591, and take a metalled drive, immediately to the left of the Windermere Hotel, signed as a footpath to Orrest Head. Walk directly uphill, ignoring turnoffs, soon taking a succession of hairpin bends through woodland. Pass a wrought-iron workshop, and walk to the top of the woods.

2 Keep right, uphill, past a trio of benches, to a metal kissing gate. A couple of inscribed stones, either side of the gate, inform you that Orrest Head was given by Arthur Henry Heywood, in 1902, to the people of Windermere.

3 Beyond the gate are steps to take you steeply up to the rocky viewpoint, with a thrilling view of the lake. Having rested your legs on one of the many benches (this is a very popular walk), continue in the same direction, picking up a grassy path downhill, towards a white farmhouse in the valley bottom. Descend through scrubland, as walls guide you towards a kissing gate next to a stile. Take the stile, and walk downhill through open pasture, with

scattered hawthorn and holly trees. Follow the wall on your left to reach a kissing gate at the bottom of the hill, to join the walled track leading, through two gates, to Causeway Farm.

(4) Turn left along the road. After 250 metres, look for a kissing gate on the left (signed 'Permissive Path'); a National Trust sign tells you this is Low Hag Wood.

(5) Take the obvious path through mostly deciduous woodland, and cross a stream on a wooden footbridge. When the path forks, keep left through a kissing gate to follow a field-edge path, with a wall to your right. At the far end of the field is another kissing gate. Continue along

If the project had gone to plan, the last section of this walk would have become the trackbed of the railway — from Windermere to Ambleside and beyond. But thanks to William Wordsworth, and other dissenting voices, Windermere is as far into the Lake District as the trains ever came.

the edge of the next field, now with a wall on your left. Keep left, following the wall along a stony track, then heading for the bottom corner of the field, to locate a kissing gate. Go back into woodland to find another kissing gate to the rear of houses.

(6) Keep left, uphill, on a path that soon narrows between walls. Cross the access drive to a house — Elleray Bank — to pick up the path again. Pass more houses and skirt woodland, with a high stone wall to the right, to emerge on the metalled drive you took at the beginning of the walk.

(7) Go right here, and back into Windermere.

Causeway Farm

19

Herdwick sheep

3 **Brant Fell and School Knott**

*A short walk linking four popular viewpoints,
each offering a subtly different view of the lake.*

With so much of the eastern shore being monopolised by grand houses, the best views of the lake can be had from the first range of fells that overlook Windermere. Our Victorian forebears knew these views too, and built 'carriage drives' up to some of the best viewpoints. The visitors who came in search of the 'sublime' and 'picturesque' could enjoy the Windermere panoramas without getting out of breath! This walk incorporates some of these carriage drives.

When visitors were first exploring the Lake District, in the latter years of the 18th century, they referred to an influential book: Thomas West's Guide to the Lakes. West listed the best 'stations and viewpoints', from which visitors could

Level:
Length: 4 miles
Terrain: Easy walking all the way
Park and start: Drive south from Bowness on the A592, in the direction of Newby Bridge. Just past the Ferry turnoff, go left along the B5284 (signed to Kendal and Lancaster). At the top of the hill, go left and immediately right (signed Kendal and Crook). After a mile, go left along Lindeth Lane. After just half a mile you'll find space on the right for half a dozen cars (GR NY415963)
Websites:
www.visitcumbria.com/amb/bowness.htm

appreciate the landscape. There were half a dozen 'stations' around Windermere, including a lodge on the lower slopes of Claife Heights (visited

(map labels:)
Old Droomer
School Knott
School Knott Tarn
Helm Road
Helm Farm
Dales Way
Brant Fell
7 8 9 6 10 5 4 13 12 2 1 11
START
B5284
Bowness
Crook →

Near School Knott Tarn

on walk 8), and the rocky outcrop of Brant Fell.

1 Walk back down the road, passing a gate and 'footpath' sign on the right. Ignore them. Just 50 metres further on, by a 'pull-in' that will fit two or three cars, there's another footpath fingerpost on the right. Walk up to a stile by a gate, to join a good path. Where the path divides, keep left, uphill, to reach the rocky outcrop of Brant Fell, which offers a glorious panorama of the lake. Directly below – though mostly hidden – is Bowness Bay, Cockshott

Point, Ferry Nab and the marina. More visible is the long thin island of Belle Isle, and the eccentric round house built on the southern end.

2 Head right, downhill, on a grassy path towards a wood, to locate a ladder stile over a wall, with a path that soon takes you to another favourite viewpoint, Post Knott, where a couple of benches command the view across the lake.

3 Take the obvious path to the right, downhill, through a kissing gate and into woodland. Join a good track – another carriage drive – leading downhill. Come to a crossroad of tracks, where you cut across the final stretch of the Dales Way (left takes you down into

Old Droomer Cottage

Bowness; turn right and, after about a week, you'd be in Ilkley).

4 Your route is straight ahead on the carriage drive, signed 'Permitted path to Helm Road', to a gate and metalled road. This is Helm Road, and your route is right, uphill (but for another splendid viewpoint over the lake, go left and almost immediately right, to take a path —

signed 'Biskey Howe').

5 Walk up Helm Road, which soon forks; your way is ahead, between a slate-built house and its garage. The track immediately forks again; keep right, following a yellow arrow along a minor metalled road, uphill. Pass a few houses (including a farmhouse – Helm Farm - with a datestone of 1691).

6 As the track swings round the farm, take a kissing gate on the left, to follow a track, with trees to your left and a fence to the right, through another kissing gate and a wall-stile. Join a track, going right, still following the fence. Skirt

houses through scrubby woodland; where the path forks, your route is acutely right, signed 'School Knott'.

Follow this path uphill, through a kissing gate, keeping to the right of Low Lickbarrow Farm. Cross a small field to a metal kissing gate and a minor road. Go right to take a wall-stile (signed 'FP to Old Droomer'), and join a field path downhill. At the bottom of the field take a ladder stile,

Last stretch

a tiny bridge made of stone slabs and up some steps to meet a track.

7 Go left, immediately bearing right by a house (this is Old Droomer Cottage). The track ends at a gate; go right and follow a sign, 'School Knott', past a commemmorative stone, through a copse of newly-planted trees.

8 Climb up to the rocky viewpoint of School Knott, which offers yet another view of Lake Windermere. Walk across the knott, keeping right to descend to School Knott Tarn.

9 Keep to the right of the tarn, to follow a path, slightly downhill, to a kissing gate. Continue on a good path, soon joining a more substantial track (this is the Dales Way).

The Dales Way is an exhilarating 87-mile walk from Ilkley to Bowness. If you meet any Dales Wayfarers on this walk, they'll be looking triumphant but footsore. Believe me, I know... and you can read all about my (mis)adventures in Dawdling Through the Dales, also from Halsgrove...

10 When you meet a T-junction of tracks, go acutely left, to continue along the Dales Way. The walking is easy, through three gates; the surface is metalled as you approach houses. The lane meets the B5284 road.

11 Your route is to the right, though a section of path has been created to save walking on the road. Where the path ends, at a gate, go right along a lane, following a Dales Way arrow and signs for Low Cleabarrow.

12 As you approach a house (this is Low Cleabarrow), go left, through a gate, still signed as the Dales Way. Follow a field-edge path to your right, downhill, through a succession of three kissing gates. After the third gate, bear right, uphill, through a stand of oak trees, through another kissing gate to meet a minor road.

13 The route ahead is clear for Dales Wayfarers, but you go left, along the road. Keep right, where the road forks, to arrive back at your car.

Windermere from Brant Fell

Ghyll Head Reservoir

4 **Rosthwaite Heights and Winster**

Another panoramic view of the lake and a visit to the lovely Winster valley

There is good walking to be had on the low-lying fells between Kendal and Lake Windermere. It's a softer landscape than the hills around the north end of the lake. Small it may be, but the River Winster used to be the boundary between the ancient counties of Lancashire and Westmorland.

It was while living in the Winster valley, between 1925 and 1932, that Arthur Ransome wrote **Swallows and Amazons**. The book featured the adventures of the Walker and Blackett children as they sailed boats, climbed mountains, panned for gold and camped on islands... all with a refreshing lack of adult supervision! The lake and landmarks Ransome described seem to have been an amalgam of Coniston, Windermere and his own fertile imagination.

Level:
Length: 4 miles
Terrain: Easy walking, mostly on good paths and tracks.

Park and start: Drive south from Bowness on the A592, for three miles. Pass a sharp right-hand bend (and junction with the B5360); 500m further on, take an unclassified road to the left (signed Ghyll Head), steeply uphill. Pass houses and park opposite Ghyll Head Reservoir; there's a pull-in that will accommodate three or four cars (GR NY399925).

Websites: The Arthur Ransome Society www.arthur-ransome.org

Map labels:
Rosthwaite Farm
A5074
Brown Horse
Winster
Rosthwaite Heights
Winster House
Ghyll Head Road
Reservoir
START
6 7 5 4 3 8 9 10 11 1

① To begin the walk you have a baffling choice of four gates — all higher than usual, to keep the deer in (or out...). No problem, just take the kissing gate to the right, signed to Black Beck and Rosthwaite, onto a path that soon brings you to another kissing gate. Keep straight ahead, with woodland on your left, as a sign tells you this is Candlestick Moss: a mixture of heathland and wetland, with scattered silver birches and knuckles of rock pushing up through the bracken.

A good level path (with a length of duckboarding to keep walkers dry-shod) brings you to another kissing gate. Then there's more duckboards and a kissing gate, as you come out onto open pasture. Here, by a lone tree, is a choice of tracks; your way is

Windermere from Rosthwaite Heights

a track to the right, downhill (signed to Rosthwaite) towards a farm in the valley (but first, if you want a delectable view of the lake, go straight on to reach Rosthwaite Heights, where a cairn and a stone bench mark the best vantage point).

2 Follow the track downhill, leap across a couple of tiny streams, and over a wall-stile, to pass the house, outbuildings and large pond of Rosthwaite Farm.

3 At the far end of the pond, bear right, signed to Winster, on a good gravel track through conifer woodland.

4 Leave the wood via another gate, to be out onto

heathland. Continue uphill on a stony track, ignoring other tracks, until you get a view into the Winster valley ahead. Head towards the white buildings, passing gorse bushes, hawthorns and silver birches. Downhill, accompanying a wall on your right,

you come to another meeting of tracks.

5 Take the gate ahead, and continue straight on. Though the path is suddenly less clear, you just follow the course of a small

Typical heathland

stream down into open pasture, with rocky outcrops and unmended walls. When the stream goes right, and disappears into a sink-hole, keep straight ahead, on a path between tumbledown walls, and through a gate to a pleasant spot by a stream. Walls create an enclosure; you can imagine sheep must have been dipped here. Courting couples must have sat here too, perhaps on the clapper bridge

Old-fashioned gatepost

Buzzards may be seen on any of these walks. They catch the thermals off the hills that descend to the lake, wheeling high up into the sky with 'ragged', upturned wingtips. You may hear buzzards before you see them; listen out for their 'mewing' cry.

made of two slabs of stone. You can imagine ladies walking to church from the nearby farms.

6 Cross the bridge and walk right, to follow a narrow path between a wall on the left and the beck on your right. The path soon broadens to a track that leads, via a gate, past a house and to a road.

7 Go right, along the road, passing the Old Post Office (with a datestone of 1600, it's one of the most photographed houses in the area) and village hall (there is room to park a few cars opposite the hall, which makes this an alternative start for the walk).

8 Round a bend to reach the Brown Horse pub, conveniently at the halfway point of the walk. The flagged stone floors, good beers and fulsome menu might just persuade you to give up the walk altogether, and settle instead for an afternoon of drunken forgetfulness. To continue the walk, take the minor road, opposite the pub, signed to Bowland Bridge and Winster Church.

The Old Post Office, Winster

9 Beyond a house called Green Yew, look for a wall-stile - and footpath sign - on the right. Follow the field edge path to another stile, next to a very old-fashioned gate: a six-barred wooden gate that slots through holes in the stone gate-posts. Cross the stile and follow the path through a wood; leave the woodland via another stile. Keep to the left edge of a field, down to cross a stream on a rather elaborate footbridge. Follow a field path uphill, now keeping a wall to your right, to locate a wall-stile (by a gate) at the top of the hill. Continue uphill to a gate, and then walk the left edge of the next field to a kissing gate giving access to a good track. Walk uphill; this is the access drive to Winster House.

10 Bear right, immediately in front of the building, onto a stony track, meandering uphill to another deer-proof gate. Soon you come to a T-junction of tracks.

11 Your route is half-left here, to join a path (look for a yellow arrow). The path offers easy, level walking through a now familiar landscape of bracken and silver birches. Beyond a gate the path continues through open scrubland - look out for deer — and delivers you back to where you parked your car.

Windermere and River Leven from Gummer's How

5 Cartmel Fell And Gummer's How

An undemanding circuit through lower Lakeland fells, visiting a beautiful old church.

St Anthony's Church at Cartmel Fell is a little gem. Hidden away from prying eyes, off a very minor road, its isolation may have saved it from the well meaning 'improvements' in Victorian times that have spoiled too many Lakeland churches. It was built in 1504, as a chapel of ease to serve the local farming community, to save them the long walk to the parish church at Cartmel. It wasn't until 1712 that marriages, baptisms and funerals could be conducted here. Incidentally, this is the only church in the north of England that is dedicated to St Anthony.

The setting is delightful – especially when viewed from the lynch-gate – and the interior is even better. Most of the stained glass is 15th century, and came from Cartmel Priory. The three decker pulpit, dated 1698, is unusual: lower deck for the clerk, middle deck for the reader, top deck for the vicar to deliver his sermon. There are two boxed pews, also inscribed with 17th century dates, where prominent local families would sit. Even the roof timbers are original.

Level: Cartmel Fell ● Gummer's How ● ●
Length: 5 miles for the circular walk to Cartmel Fell; 1 ½ miles for Gummer's How
Terrain: mostly easy walking on open terrain. The last section to Gummer's How is short... but steep.
Park and start: From the roundabout near Newby Bridge, take the A592 north. After 1km, bear right, opposite Fell Foot Park, and take the unclassified road, steeply uphill. Park, towards the top of the hill, in the Gummer's How Forestry Commision car park (GR SD389877).
Websites: more about St Anthony's Church at Cartmel Fell
www.lancashirechurches.co.uk/cartmelfell.htm

Sow How Tarn

down to Sow How Tarn.

1 Walk up the road: a steep pull to the top of the hill, with woodland either side, then gently downhill.

2 As you come to the end of Chapel House Wood, take the first road on the right, Sow How Lane.

3 Walk through the farmyard of Sow How Farm, to continue on a good track. At a fork of tracks, 100m past the farm, bear left, through open pasture, and a gate,

4 Keep to the main track and cross a small beck. Follow the track uphill to a gate and into woodland. Ignore a footpath on the left, and keep to the track; leave the woodland via another gate. Follow the wall to your right, as the track bears sharply right, to pass Heights Cottage: living accomodation and space for livestock, under one roof... but now looking rather delapidated.

5 Walk downhill, between walls, to a gate that gives onto open pasture (known as Raven's Barrow). Enjoy views ahead to Whitbarrow Scar, to the right Morecambe Bay, and to the left the Howgill fells. The track soon forks;

keep left (on the less prominent track), crest the hill and walk downhill. Your track becomes clearer and leads down, via a gate, to a road.

6 Walk right, along the road, until it forks.

7 Instead of deciding which fork to take, look for a path on the left, along the edge of woodland, signed as a footpath to St Anthony's Church. You enter the churchyard by a wall-stile, and, once you've taken a look at this wonderfully sited old church (don't forget to go inside...) your route is to retrace your steps to the fork in the road. Cross the road to take a ladder stile, to join a grassy track uphill to a wall-stile. Ignore the path to the right, going steeply uphill;

St Andrew's Church, Cartmel Fell

keep straight ahead, on the level, to another ladder stile. Walk straight through Rankin's Plantation, re-emerging from the dense conifer woodland via a gate.

8 Your way is ahead, on a grassy track, through a typical South Lakeland landscape of bracken and scrubland. Your path is

Interior with box-pews

At 313 metres, Gummer's How offers the highest viewpoint over the southern reaches of the lake. Below is the quay at Lakeside, where the pleasure steamers dock, before heading off to the fleshpots of Bowness and Waterhead. It's hard to call them anything but 'steamers,' though the three classic craft – Swan, Teal and Tern – were long since converted to diesel power.

Trig point on top of Gummer's How

joined by a more substantial track. Go through a gate onto a track defined by dry stone walls. At the top of a rise, bear sharp left (following a yellow arrow). Continue uphill to meet a very minor road. Go right, soon passing a

knot of houses – Foxfield – as the road is downgraded to a farm track.

9 Through a gate you walk in open pasture, interspersed with rocky outcrops. Beyond another gate, your path is clear: back to Sow How Farm, along Sow How Lane, left at the T-junction and back to the Gummer's How car park.

Gummer's How

Walk up the road for just 100m, and take a gate on the left, to join a good track through scrub and woodland. The path gets steeper as you climb Gummer's How; you can carry on straight ahead, or take a path to the right which may be easier for old or weary legs. Either way, the view from the top is ample reward. Your return route is simple: it's the way you came!

6 Finsthwaite Heights and High Dam

Another 'two for the price of one' walk: exploring the woods above Lakeside and a site of local industry.

Level: Finsthwaite Heights 🐾🐾 High Dam 🐾

Length: Finsthwaite Heights 3 miles; circuit of High Dam 1 ¼ miles

Terrain: The usual ups and downs; nothing too strenuous.

Park and start: Pass the Swan Hotel at Newby Bridge, at the bottom of the lake, and drive past Lakeside. Go left at Stott Park Bobbin Mill, then left again. Just before you come into the village of Finsthwaite, follow signs on the right to High Dam car park (GR SD368882).

Websites: Consider combining this walk with a visit to Stott Park Bobbin Mill, now in the custody of English Heritage www.english-heritage.org.uk

Windermere isn't quite the rural idyll that visitors often imagine it to be. Wherever a stream could be dammed and diverted, the water was used to turn a waterwheel. There were many mills in the area, though most were on a smaller scale than in the towns. There were, for example, 60 bobbin mills in South Lakeland — producing bobbins from coppiced woodland to supply the burgeoning cotton industry of Lancashire. Stott Park Bobbin Mill, near Lakeside, opened in 1835 and turned its last bobbin as recently as 1971. It has since been reopened, by English Heritage, as a working museum.

Stott Park needed a steady supply of water to power the lathes, but the flow from the beck was irregular. So, to maintain a good 'head' of water, the beck was dammed to create a pair of reservoirs, High Dam and Low Dam.

Water was carried, via a complex arrangement of leats and culverts, down to the waterwheel at the mill.

Finsthwaite Tower

Finsthwaite Tower

Finsthwaite Tower was 'erected to honour the officers, seamen and marines of the Royal Navy, whose matchless conduct and irresistible valour decisively defeated the fleets of France, Spain and Holland' in 1799. But, like the navy itself, Finsthwaite Tower has seen better days.

Around a bobbin-shaped sculpture, at High Dam car park, is this inscription: "This is the water that turns the wheel, that spins the lathe, that shapes the wood, to make the bobbin, to wind the thread, that wove the wealth of Lancashire. These are the trees, that cut by man, will sprout again, feed Stott Mill, to make the bobbins to earn the pay, that fed the folk of Finsthwaite".

1 Walk back down to the road; go right, into the village of Finsthwaite. Take a lane on the left, to pass St Peter's Church and the village hall, to a gate where the lane ends.

2 Follow the obvious track across a field to another gate. The track stops, but your route is straight ahead, across the next field, to locate a wall-stile.

Finsthwaite Church

Newby Bridge

 3 Join a good path uphill through woodland, which forks almost immediately. Take the lesser fork, to the right, uphill, keeping right as you meet a forestry track. The track climbs steadily through a mixture of broadleaved and conifer trees. Keep right when the track forks; at the top of a rise, take a path to the right (look for a white arrow) through a gap in a wall. The path undulates through more open woodland; towards the top of the hill you will come to Finsthwaite Tower on Summer House Knott, half hidden amongst the trees.

4 Continue in the same direction you were walking before you made a detour to the tower: an obvious path downhill, through a gap in a wall (another slight detour, soon after, offers a view of the River Leven from a rocky outcrop). Continue downhill — so steeply that stone steps have been made — through woodland, to a gate. Here the path narrows, between fences, and comes out to meet an access track (for refreshments, go left here, cross the railway line, to find the Swan Inn at Newby Bridge).

Through the woods...

Herdwick sheep

(5) Go right, along the track; where it ends, between a house and its outbuildings, carry straight ahead, uphill, on a woodland path. Beyond a stile it's a steep pull uphill; when the path levels out, leave the wood via a gap in a wall.

(6) Cross three fields (keeping to the right in the second one, to keep your feet dry), as the quaint tower of Finsthwaite Church comes into view. Go through a kissing gate, to arrive back in Finsthwaite. Go right along the road, and left, beyond the village, to return to the High Dam car park.

High Dam

The walk to High Dam is a popular one, for which no route-finding skills are required. Beyond the little sculpture, showing the area in relief, take the obvious track uphill through deciduous woodland. Keep the beck to your left and you'll soon reach Low Dam and, a little further uphill, High Dam.

There's a path all the way round High Dam, with footbridges to take you across the becks that feed into the reservoir. When you've completed the circuit of the tarn, retrace your steps back down to the car park.

High Dam

7 Sawrey and Rawlinson Nab

A circuit around the landscape that was so familiar to Beatrix Potter, finishing with a stroll along the lake shore.

Level: 🐾
Length: 5 miles
Terrain: For a few days each year the shoreline section of this walk will be impossible, when the lake is high. Don't worry... unless it's been raining for days...
Park and start: Ash Landing car park, on the B5285 between Far Sawrey and the Ferry, on the western side of the lake (GR SD388954). If coming from Bowness, take the ferry.
Websites: Consider combining this walk with a visit to Beatrix Potter's house at Hill Top, Near Sawrey www.nationaltrust.org.uk

The western side of Windermere is an area that Beatrix Potter knew well. From the proceeds of her children's books – 23 in all, beginning with **The Tale of Peter Rabbit** - she bought Hill Top, in Near Sawrey. As her fame grew, she acquired a number of farms too, which she eventually left to the National Trust.

Her literary output gradually diminished. She married William Heelis, a local solicitor, and developed a passion for breeding and showing Herdwick sheep, a hardy Lakeland breed. She may have been well-known around the world, but to local people she was a farmer and a judge at the agricultural shows. Children knew the rotund, dishevelled figure as 'Old Mother Heelis'. She came to resemble Mrs Tiggy-Winkle, one of her own characters.

Beatrix Potter died in Sawrey, in 1943. Her books have survived well, and all

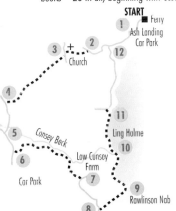

START
Ferry
Ash Landing
Car Park
1
2
3 +
Church
12
4
11
5 Cunsey Beck
Ling Holme
10
6
Low Cunsey
Farm
7
Car Park
9 Rawlinson Nab
8

remain in print. Hill Top is now a literary shrine on a par with William Wordsworth and Dove Cottage, and is particularly popular with Japanese visitors. Bizarrely, an exact replica of Hill Top has been recreated at a children's zoo in Tokyo!

St Peter's Church, Sawrey

1 From Ash Landing car park follow the road uphill (or, rather, the path that runs parallel, first on the right of the road, then on the left). A little road walking is required,

past two road junctions on the left, to the top of the hill. Go left, at the top, immediately after a pair of semi-detached cottages, to take a narrow path between a fence and a wall.

2 Beyond a kissing gate, you are out into open fields, with your immediate destination – St Peter's Church – in the valley below. Keep right, following a wall downhill, across a couple of fields, and pass to the left of the churchyard to reach a road.

3 Go left here, and, after a few metres, turn right at a kissing gate just after Dove Cottage (no, not that one...). Guided by a yellow arrow, cross a beck and take a track that follows a line of trees. The field narrows to a stile; continue in the same

Road through the woods

direction, through a gate and, soon after, a kissing gate on the right. Walk to the far end of a long field to another kissing gate and into woodland. Ignore the path to the right; your route is straight ahead, gently downhill. Cross duckboards over a boggy section, your path getting steeper as you join a broader track, that comes down, via a pair of gates, to a road.

4 Walk left along this minor road, cross Cunsey Beck, to meet another road by a cottage.

Windermere from Rawlinson Nab

5 Go left here. Where the road bears right, uphill, and fields give way to woodland, take a track on the left (signed as a bridlway to Cunsey).

6 Enjoy easy, level walking, through deciduous woodland, with Cunsey Beck burbling away to your left. When the track forks, bear right, away from the beck, to meet a road by Low Cunsey Farm.

7 Walk right, along the road; immediately before some farm buildings, take a stile and stone steps on the left.

In full sail on a glassy lake

8 A path takes you down to the lake shore.

9 You soon arrive at a small shingle beach: a popular sun-trap in summer for people who arrive both on foot and by boat. Just beyond

the beach is a small promontory – Rawlinson Nab - crowned with trees and a strategically sited bench. You can admire some of the large houses on the opposite shore of the lake. Few are grander than Storrs Hall: unusual in having a prime, south-facing position.

10 Beyond a stile you pass a small island – Ling Holme – just

Rawlinson Nab was one of Thomas West's 'stations', where visitors to the Lake District might avail themselves of a particularly fine view. The views are pleasant rather than dramatic, but none the worse for that.

offshore. Take a footbridge across Cunsey Beck: one of the larger of the many watercourses that drain into the lake. Negotiate a stile as you pass a couple of boathouses; after the next stile you're in open pasture. Pass behind a property – the Bield, a house and boathouse combined – to meet a road.

11 Go right, along the road, in pleasantly wooded surroundings, while easing away from the lake. Beyond the drive to Bryers Cottage the road climbs uphill. After two whitewashed houses, take the road to the right, downhill, soon joining the road that leads to the ferry.

12 Follow the path adjacent to the road, to make your way back down to the car park at Ash Landing.

8 Claife Heights

Climb the wooded flanks on the western shore of the lake, with views of Bowness Bay at its best... from a distance.

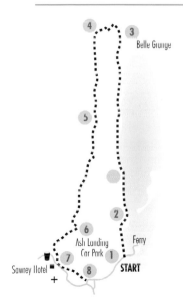

Level: ♦♦
Length: 5 ½ miles
Terrain: level walking by the lake, level walking across Claife Heights, with a short steep section in between.
Park and start: Take the B5285 from Far Sawrey to the ferry (or cross the lake by ferry). Park in Ash Landing car park (GR SD388954, as for walk 7), or take the road from close to the ferry along the lake shore, where there is another pay & display car park (and, further on, free parking).
Websites: Claife Heights and viewing station www.visitcumbria.com/amb/claife.htm

Windermere is one of the most artificially enhanced valleys in the Lake District, though this isn't immediately obvious. At the time William Wordsworth was born, in 1770, the slopes on the western side of the lake would have been almost bare. The trees had been cleared, during previous centuries, to create sheep pasture. The Enclosures Acts of the 19th century brought a lot of these fells into private ownership, and the new landowners were keen to make their mark on the landscape, in the most literal kind of way.

John Curwen, who lived in the eccentric 'round house' on Belle Isle, planted 30,000 larch trees on Claife Heights, mostly for aesthetic reasons.

Quiet mooring near the ferry

Other landowners followed his lead, which changed the Windermere landscape, probably for the better.

1 From Ash Landing car park, walk towards the ferry, before taking a road to the left, which follows the lakeshore, going north, with grassy pasture on the left.

2 After a cattle grid, the road enters National Trust woodland – coniferous and broadleaved – and becomes a stony track (no cars allowed beyond this point), which makes a detour to pass Strawberry Gardens, a small caravan park. Pass a boathouse on the right and approach a white house – Belle Grange - to find a three-way finger post.

At the back of Belle Isle

Make mine a pint

3 Go left, signed as 'Bridleway to Hawkshead', on a paved track which, remarkably, was once the main road from Kendal to Hawkshead, using a ferry that ran from Millerground to Belle Grange. The 'engineered' track climbs steeply uphill, through woodland, until you come to a junction of paths.

4 Go left here, leaving the paved track by taking a tiny stream in a single athletic bound, and continuing uphill on a stony path. When the path forks, keep right, to follow a yellow arrow, still uphill. As the path levels off you're effectively walking along a grassy 'terrace', with intermittent views of the lake to your left. Follow another yellow arrow through a gap in the wall to your right, as the path continues through thick conifer woodland. You lose the lake views as the path leads downhill and is soon enclosed by mossy walls.

5 Leave the woods via a gate; at the top of a rise you join a more substantial track. Continue downhill, with fields to your left and conifer woodland to your right, through a gate and out into open fields. Pass to the left of a small tarn, and continue downhill on the walled track, to a sort of paddock, surrounded by walls and fences, and a three-way finger-post. Left is a short-cut back to the ferry and your car park; right is signed to Hill Top and Sawrey.

6 Go right, along the good track, downhill, with Beatrix Potter's village, Near Sawrey, in the middle distance. That pint looks a long way away. Fortunately, the track leads directly down to the Sawrey Hotel; you and your walking boots will be welcome in the Claife Crier bar.

7 To continue the walk, take a cinder track bearing left, at

the far end of the hotel car park, signed 'Ferry via Ash Landing'. Pass houses, and go through a metal kissing gate. Cross the drive of a house, Sawrey Knotts, and follow the path ahead, onto a metalled track. Pass stables, through another metal kissing gate, as your path follows a wall on your right. The lake comes into view once again. Cross an access road, to join a walled track downhill and then the road that leads to the ferry.

Robin offering guidance at Belle Grange

and back to Ash Landing car park. There's one more thing to see, however, so take the path that continues at the far side of the car park. Walk uphill to the ruins of Claife Station which, hopefully, will one day be in better condition than it is at present.

8 Go left, down the road (or the path that runs parallel to it)

Claife Station
This lodge, now in a rather ruinous state, is another of the 'stations' that offered especially fine views of the lake, through bay windows on two floors. In an effort to 'improve' on Nature, and imitate seasonal changes, each pane of glass was a different colour. Light green glass simulated spring, yellow was for summer and orange for autumn, while light blue gave the scene the chilly hues of winter. A dark blue window bathed the scene in 'moonlight'; another had a liliac tinge to suggest a thunderstorm!

Mossy woodland

9 **Wray Castle and Latterbarrow**

Start and finish at an example of architectual eccentricity, and enjoy great views across the lake.

While some of the houses around the lake were built with some sensitivity to their surroundings, others **START** stick out like the proverbial sore thumb. Before the creation of the national park, and a tightening up of planning regulations, men of great wealth, but limited taste, were able to indulge their wildest architectural fantasies.

Imagine a castle drawn by an inventive 7-year-old, and imagine an architect using this fanciful drawing as a blueprint. Actually, there's no real need to imagine it, because here it is in all its gothic, mock-medieval glory. Wray Castle — complete with battlements and arrow-slits — was built in the 1840s for James Dyson, a retired surgeon from Liverpool. Both incongruous and anachronistic, Wray Castle was nevertheless one of the few buildings around the lake to earn William Wordsworth's approval!

Level: 🐾 🐾
Length: 5 miles
Terrain: A steep climb up to the viewpoint of Latterbarrow then an easy walk along the lake shore.
Park and start: From Ambleside take the A593, signed to Coniston, Hawkshead and Langdale. At the first community, Clappersgate, go left onto the B5286, signed to Hawkshead. After a couple of miles, bear left onto an unclassified road, signed to Wray Castle. Beyond the entrace to Low Wray Campsite is an elaborate gatehouse; go through it to reach Wray Castle. Park at the back of the building
Websites: More about Wray Castle
www.visitcumbria.com/nattrust/wray.htm

Map labels:
- Wray Castle 1
- 2
- High Wray Bay 8
- High Wray 3
- Basecamp 4
- Latterbarrow 5
- 6
- Belle Grange 7

The battlements of Wray Castle

1 Walk back down the drive, beneath the crenellated arch of the gatehouse, and turn left along this quiet road.

2 Walk up to the tiny community of High Wray (above the houses looms the bulk of Latterborrow, your immediate destination). Beyond where a road bears off left (signed to the ferry) is a track, also on the left, with a sign, 'Basecamp'.

Ambleside seen from Latterbarrow

3 Take this track uphill, passing the entrance to Basecamp (an outdoor centre run by the National Trust) and through a gate.

4 When the track bears left, look out on the right for a path that leads to a stile and into deciduous woodland. Leave the wood via a kissing gate to join a path that gets ever steeper, through bracken and scattered trees.

The cairn on Latterbarrow

5 Soon you reach the top of Latterbarrow. Turn round to look at the view: the northern expanse of the lake, and Ambleside, cradled by Loughrigg Fell, Fairfield, Red Screes and Wansfell, with a backdrop of higher peaks.

Having enjoyed the view, bear right, to the cairn. While some Lakeland

A steam launch makes stately progress

summits are marked by a pile of rocks, Latterbarrow boasts a structure of height and craftsmanship. Bear slightly left from the cairn, to take a broad, grassy track downhill. Cross a stile and bear sharp left, into conifer woodland, offering level walking on a carpet of pine needles.

When you leave the wood, via a gap in a wall, your way is not immediately clear — due to the extensive tree-felling (all part of the life-cycle of

The first written evidence of a ferry across Windermere dates back to 1454, with nothing in the account to suggest that this was a new venture. The ferry crossed the lake at its narrowest point, from Ferry Nab to the Ferry Inn. On one tragic night in 1635 the ferry sank with a wedding party from Hawkshead on board, killing 47 passengers.

Another ferry ran from Millerground, on the eastern shore of the lake, to Belle Grange on the west. This route formed part of what was once the 'main road' linking the market towns of Kendal and Hawkshead. The ferryman's house can still be seen at Millerground; a bell, in a tiny belfry on the gable end of the cottage, was rung if the ferry needed to be summoned from Belle Grange.

conifer woodland, though it looks rather bare right now). Walk straight ahead for 50m, then your path turns right, slightly uphill. When you meet a wall, keep right, uphill; at a hole in the wall take steps, left, downhill to

walk up to another wall gap, where you leave the scene of woodland devastation behind.

6 At a T-junction of tracks, your route is left, signed as

'Bridleway to the Ferry and Far Sawrey'. You meet a broad forestry track, but your way is straight ahead, signed 'Belle Grange'. This unassuming path was once the main highway between the market towns of Kendal and Hawkshead. Your way is gently downhill through mixed woodland, as you cross another forestry track. In places you'll see your path has been 'engineered' to keep a steady gradient; parts of the track are still paved. At a junction of tracks, you carry straight on downhill to meet the lake shore at a house called Belle Grange.

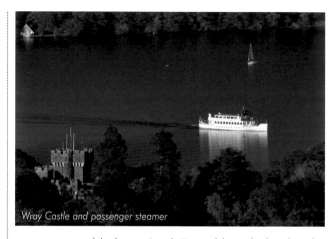

Wray Castle and passenger steamer

(7) Join the broad track going left, to follow the lake shore. Beyond a gate with big stone gate-posts, bear right, through a car park, to continue on a path by the water's edge. The walking is easy, crossing tiny streams that empty into the lake, through deciduous woodland.

 Pass High Wray Bay, with its pair of matching boat-houses.

Your track leaves the shore, but only briefly; take a gate on your right (signed 'Wray Castle') and walk through pasture. At a dead tree by the water's edge, bear left, uphill, back to the battlements of Wray Castle.

10 Loughrigg Fell and Grasmere

Loughrigg Fell is a walkers' playground, with ever-changing views of Windermere, Grasmere and Rydal Water

Level: 🥾 🥾 🥾
Length: 6 miles
Terrain: some steep sections. Be sure to pack your OS map
Park and start: Leave Ambleside by the A593, signed to Hawkshead and Langdale. Immediately beyond the humpback bridge over the River Rothay, turn right on an unclassified road. Park a mile up this road, near Miller Bridge (GR NY371046). Or park in Ambleside and walk through Rothay park to Miller Bridge.
Websites: www.amblesideonline.co.uk

On this walk you get a taste of the bigger Lakeland hills. The view from the far side of Loughrigg Fell offers up an impressive frieze of peaks and valleys. You also become acquainted with two other, smaller, expanses of water – Grasmere and Rydal Water and, if you know where to look, two of the houses where William Wordsworth lived.

On his return to the Lake District in 1799, Wordsworth set up home with his sister Dorothy, at Dove Cottage, on the edge of Grasmere village. He married his childhood companion, Mary Hutchinson, in 1802, and the first three of their five children were born here. It was at Dove Cottage that he produced what was arguably his best work. The Wordsworth family rented Rydal Mount, a more substantial property, from 1813 onwards. Both

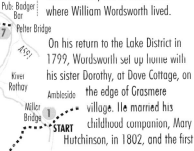

properties — and the Dove Cottage Museum — are now open to the public.

1 Walk past Miller Bridge, spanning the River Rothay. Beyond a cattle grid, go left up a metalled lane, signed as a public bridleway. When the lane bears left, beyond a couple of houses, go right, over a wall stile, onto a path that fringes woodland. After a gate, and a footbridge over a beck, you are out on the open fell. Your path forks here; keep right, steeply uphill (there are steps to help you) and keep climbing until your path levels out.

2 Carry on until you reach Lily Tarn (at this point it's worth the effort of climbing the rocky

Miller Bridge

Miller Bridge spans the River Rothay when it is joined by Stock Beck. Though it has the appearance of an ancient packhorse bridge, it was actually a replacement for another bridge that was washed away by floodwater in 1899.

outcrops to your left, because they afford some wonderful views directly up the lake). Keep to the right of the tarn, and continue on a good path ahead, using the Langdale Pikes as a rough guide, through typical Lakeland terrain: bracken, rocks, crags, tiny streams and a bewildering network of paths. Before long you'll be seeing

Loughrigg Tarn, rather bigger than Lily Tarn, down to your left, and the River Brathay and Elter Water further down in the valley.

There's no point trying to provide a particular route here. Loughrigg Fell is great for walkers because it is criss-crossed with paths. It's bad for writers of walking books for the very same reason. Anyway, if you're going to get lost, then Loughrigg Fell is the ideal place to do it (and to hone your map-reading skills). A crag with a cairn on top appears at first sight to be the highest point on Loughrigg Fell, but it's not.

3 Continue straght ahead; the trig point — the highest piont of this walk — is on top of the next crag. The view from the trig point is

View over Grasmere from the Loughrigg Fell

Herdwick... and a last glimpse of the lake

well worth the walk; this is a good spot to eat your sandwiches and drink in the view. Down below is Grasmere, both the village and the lake, with the Langdales, the Coniston range, Fairfield, Dunmail Raise towards Helvellyn, and, still, a view of Windermere behind you.

From the trig point your route is to head for the left side of Grasmere lake; pick up a path that descends steeply into the valley. As you approach woodland, you meet a cinder track.

(**4**) Go right here – this is Loughrigg Terrace – and enjoy easy, level walking with ever-changing views of Grasmere. Keep right, when another path joins yours; soon you have another choice.

Miller Bridge, Ambleside

have easy walking — even easier when, after cottages, the track becomes metalled. (Opposite the second group of houses is a gate on the left. This a short-cut, via a footbridge across the River Rothay, to the Badger Bar in Rydal, where beer and sandwiches await). If you're not visiting the pub, just carry on past the cottages, and Pelter Bridge car park, to a road junction by Pelter Bridge itself.

5 Left is down to Rydal Water, but you go right, on a well-made track.

6 The purpose of this track is soon apparent, as you reach Rydal Cave: not a natural feature of the landscape, in fact, but a long-abandoned slate quarry (as indicated by the spoil heaps nearby). Follow the path downhill from the cave; after a couple of hairpin bends you're in woodland, then almost to the shore of Rydal Water. Through a gate, you

7 Don't cross the bridge; bear right here, along a road (for vehicles it's 'access only', so you'll see little traffic). It's easy walking, along the flat, following the course of the River Rothay, back to Miller Bridge and your car.

The gloomy interior of Rydal Cave